Published by Polari Press
polari.com @polaripress

ISBN: 978-1-914237-09-6

Printed by Severn Print using vegetable
inks on Munken White 90gsm paper.
Typeset in 10/12 Roslindale.

Cover design and typesetting
by Peter Collins for Polari.

This first edition was printed in
the UK in October 2022.

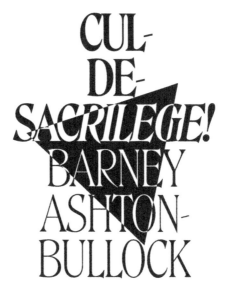

CUL-DE-SACRILEGE!

BARNEY ASHTON-BULLOCK

(Up 'em Queer Byways...)

polari

CONTENTULARS!

introit-ish...

a sensu-sexual, intra-spatial, impressionistic poem tract of outsider queerdom. tracing a trajectory of florid trauma from rural childhood where hope of connection sprang eternal, via the formative cataclysmic loneliness of a queer rural Dorset youthdom and the last days of school, via leaving for the promissory distant promiscuities of the city, via the unsatisfactory anonymous encounters and thwarted unrequited loves thereof, via first jobs, the sexual exploitations wrought of naïvety, sub/dom relationships gone *wrong* to the misplaced consolatory coping strategy of illicit drug addiction, societal lockdown, armageddon and its waif & wastrel, reductive aftermath.

fronded throughout by tender recollections of an idealised past and by the curative fantasies of escapism, this is one queer Everyman's journey; not a story *per se* but a sequence of poetic stall-wall etchings of desperation from the staging posts of an pedestrian life upon which psycho-geographies graft upon psycho-geographies in synchronicity to the pending Armageddon; a troubled trajectory and a testament to queer survival and its workaday hurts; pre and post-*enfrazzlement*!

intro : scab-ble

Could I prefix the word 'daisy' with the stem *'fucksa-'*, as in *'fucksadaisy'*? Is that permissible within the lexical rubric? Or, perhaps, but as a single word, *'fucksomen'*, even *'fucksamen'*, or, new word alert, *'fucksodus'*, as in bomb-rushing out the portals of a burning brothel or, perhaps, to get to the meat of the matter, *Y-A-double L*, *'yall'*, as a butted up suffix to *'fuck'* resulting in 'fuckyall' – a casual enjambment of the popular vernacular imperative, *'fuck y'all'*?

Butser Fuck

Fingers thrilled to drill the chisel into the shit-pot
   partition's veneer
And schuck out the customary 'fuck' as suffix to the name
   of the locale
Of whichever such school outing it just happened to be...

Longleat Fuck... Marwell Fuck... Tate Fuck... Tussard's
   Fuck... Butser Fuck...

Verbiage vernac - subtle as a happy slap
Such branded tag-thwack, selfied for posterity

Bag search – graffer caught – trip cut short
Soon back on the London Orb – *"miss, oh miss, I need a piss!"*
Fleet Services! Fleet Services! An' a quick stop group suck
   o'cig...

Then moonie farts from rear coach seats
Arse'oles pressed 'gainst steamy glass
The unhallowed stench of a rando follow through
Smulched on concatenated, bright orange, stay-press
   curtains
Group punishments meted, the callow grasses bleated
The ringleaders got beatz on the hard shoulder

*"Mandy got fingered under a hasty convened
blanket of blazers just past the Rownham services"*

And we drifted into chuckling complicity as she wanked to
   completion
Some ruddy-faced rugby lad who largely suppressed
An untoward ecstatic moan into a single rogue intoned,
Oddly am-dram corny porn, *"Woo-hoooo!"*

Followed by *"Oi! You got any tissues?"*
And we, all a-snigger, chimed *"No!"*

"Sniff this!" he'd later say as the evidence of the day
The whiff was modally piss but with hints of fish
and diesel on his injuncted 'c**ty finger'; *cr-cr-cringe!*

Six of the best for the starburst of mess around the zip-fly
    of his pegs
Sir not impressed by indiscreet stains of same wiped on
    the coach seat

Such marks in which we, then, neither cared nor dared
To read in the flecks of our own pasts or futures...

Fog Service Now Operating

lichen soporific *(tarty in mottly, saturate sheen)*,
spongoid planks pimpled with rot *(fecund fungi a-bop)*,
bolts shearing in sheer rust *(oxides in ochre flakery)*
and is the 'sbestos pagoda locked?

shall we 'ammer an 'ole so t'hunch 'pon't bench within?
is the train still late?
does the absence of track mean anything?
in 30-ish mins, i can walk t'Yeovil:
if you want a smutch 'n' chomp of mayoed chips,
i'm your (nearly-man) man –

if, in this landlock,
we're apprentices of the pretence that life'll give
these tender queer years, in retrospect, some scrim of
   rosey glow,
if there'd be a future in which i'd know
more about boys and what they give, or do not, freely –

you'd been furtive 'touchy-feely' on that youth retreat
and though the moments gone, we'll still meet
'til we sit our last A-levs an' bound or limp
into our fugue and flay of gayer future –

i've a job of sorts lined up in Trowbridge
and, if you work there too,
i'll give you a lift on the moped i'll steal;
we can scrump the apples, but that don't make cider –

is this blight of halt a request stop?
is this a draize of flunken days,
if there ain't any trains?
my tatter-fraz school unif in damp, drear, clung malaise,
jus'a week an' five days 'til the last e'er school bus
drops us off togeth or, e'er on, doth separate us –

'til then, let's chew the cadged cig-ends
an' swank in t'uplift of a filched tin or two
in obscured view o'the tell-tale Vale
from this knotweed riven knoll o'wringing rot,
our *'en plein air'* auberge, our den, our haunt,
our proxy, late-teen 'home from home'
where, perchance, we'll soon enough admit
that neither will trains depart again,
nor will we e'er, henceforth, 'ere loiter 'n' loll
togeth, that's for sure, but probs ne'er e'en alone –

for afore the pending wend o'clarity,
the burnin' o'the platform timbers bestow
to disperse the treacly trysts of mist,
ev'ry bloody thing, our pally platonics thus far've known,
is so soon, too soon, smutched to 'outgrown'

top atop

we bunked the high-school's last pontifical high-mass and
found a mossy rot tor of junked old desks, warped veneers
sheering like butterfly cakes, their varnish cracked to ash
atop archival graf-tag curses; *"x, y and z are fukkin' queers!"*

we toked a shared *Consulate*,
you kissed me in a lilt of threnody.
you felt *"cool as a mountain stream"*;
you'd read it on the carton,
as our school days reached their fag-end.
we heard, in the drowse of distance,
the canticle chaw as our jaws
slawed demur sexual intent

before kissing dick-dish deep again.
the sanctus bells trilled their set-piece
transubstantiation altar-top textbook
miracle as we merged into one divinity
atop the skewered discard loll of desks
and were mutually reborn in a viscous riptide
of spermy *'aspergus deo'* queer redemption,
my saint-stretched, blessed, doused ass psalming
its all new blessed anoint of *"Allelulia!"* etc.

i see your *Times* obituary did not take pause to flatter me

In my compendia of ephemera,
is a mouldering memoranda
mock injuncting us spendthrift,
ligger, domestic staff
for supping the trifle brandy
as *"trashy and traitorous behaviour"*
deserving of the lash which,
of course, you were not permitted to give,
but transgressors, when caught,
would have 'dead of night' escort
for a skinny-dip in the cesspits of shit
shat by his laughing Lordship.
I think you dunked me in '71...

In an arcana of side-room railwayana
is a tattered timetable.
Marked up on a sebum smeared page,
amongst that powdering, well-thumbed,
dog-eared mound of tome,
are train times to a long closed
branch-line's wayside halt adjacent to
the swanky public school you decanted to
from which you wrote atrophies
of promises that never took flight;
'a passing phase', the *'excuse du jour'*,
once you took vicar's counsel and took fright.
I think you dumped me in '63...

You met me a couple of times from the train;
the first time, you kissed me behind
the platform's pagoda, the second time,
you shook my hand and said,
"It's not you, it's me; this cannot be!"
the third and fourth and fifth times,
you never came to see this, then, boy

whom, for a fleeting 'once upon...',
was your consommé of everything.
Oh yes, you dumped me in the January...

British Railways Western Region pocket timetable,
coffee and drooly spittle spattered,
etched with *noms de plume* and notes that gloat
of suitors wanting and waiting
at random, remote rail-motor halts
for mutual, discreet relief
and pages ripped out, therefrom,
that'd wiped the seats
of unhitched britches
we wore when, so freshly filled
in such fresh-ish fields
of our young-ish, queerer, sophomore years.
The trains' guards, in rapt obeyance of semaphore signals
showed scant disdain for our stained flannels
as they flag-waved all those long-lost, local trains away
just as Lord Beeching, that bitter shit, did his bit,
afore the abeyance of all those lives and secondary lines.
Yes, I think I lastly had you in August '65...

alistair longtime

the coiling crampon boil
of the stinging flare of glare,
it's there, as 'ex' prefaces 'mate'
in a wired, wiry teen's accusational eyes,
our respective mental moats abrim with testiness.
appalled, we squalled to survive;
we could not paddle in such infinite gyre,
the distancing between us meant everything.

we surfed the drifting sift
as innocent childhood atrophised and atomised
through all the variegations of descent
from inseparable to despise
as the ascendency of 'maybe more'
did the reverse of pacify!
my lobbed, vaunting dream, mere lop-side,
like a dark paralysis smutching the splish-sploshery
of youth's balmy bathing waters
in seemingly eternal cinematic summers;
yet, as i lastly doggy paddled across
ever choppier seas with my enthused, ecstatic grin,
you saw a tempest storm abrew
within your own tidal ides of sin
and, though you were the lifeboat,
you would not let me in.

bobbing in disenchanted aplomb thirty years on,
still I bear the self-same barbaric,
possessive, shit-shooting, slot o'mouth,
as ever, so defensively, name-droppingly atrill,
rippling its vulgar, passive-aggressive chancery
and, as the master-poet in his masterclass splonks on
of clarity, precision, concision and form, i just hurt;
a dilettante 'poet in residence' anchored in conch
'neath hutched-up, serried bombs of long gone yesteryears.

for every fledgling is as wrappety-wrung,
eyeless of its own mortality:
i, immured in ideals of you loving me,
exclusively and queerly in perpetuity
would coalesce in this veneration of you
to be merely meted your revulsions
to feed my compulsive search for the energy of love
and a deeper quest to meet that me
I'd yet to know, lest be!

I lay latent at full stretch
beneath a compartment train seat,
bestilled for the 5 minutes to Branksome
in order, I'd hoped, to surprise you into forgiveness,
but, you saw me hiding
which amplified the stalkerish strangeness
and my cream C&A
jeans were camou-befilthed by tobacco ash
and mastic cola-dreg stained from spilt-slops
and my Swatch scuffed
and you looked at me with flummoxed hate,
not the required, requited love;
"What do you want now, bender?
I'm gonna go an' see m'Nana Branksome
She's family, you fag, and you cannot come".

You then spat phlegm in my face.
It was an approximation of dramatic disgust
that you'd once seen on *The Bill*;
a re-enactment of a thuggy, flobbing
at a bunny-boiler, boyfy clinger trope
who'd also clung too long to see
the many other junctions up which
many more scenic-routed trains
could and would, in time, have gone.

The Unashamed Dead

Would that the shamed dead forget their wretched passing?
For, from the Jezebel's tower, a curative chromatico
of songs of '*Satires Of Circumstance*' waft like a latterday
wad o'wonga in bold spectral manifest of curative effect.

Like '*Peter's Pence*' dispensed as an elixir of
miraculous absolution for the comely gone who,
long deflowered, fell in the tarry, feathered,
plough furrows, yet, now, are intact again
as effortlessly as if they'd pulled up their
askew knickers over askance legs back to the
snug, dewy tufts of their turf-downed truss;
unmowed, unmoved, unknown.

And, yonder, the meek milk maid, too, is freshly unruined
as deftly as the emptying of her hefty pail, for that sadistic
Squire's son was madhand 'transported' o'er the Ridgeway
by lanterned slatterns, aflame in their all-new corrective
    collective.

And, thus, so much promise that'd come undone is restitched
into time immemorial to bloom, jointly and severally,
'mongst lovers, 'mongst friends in reimagined life stories
erased of the plunging vacui of trauma;

And, yet, for that, I be the second grandson of that
second son, that twisted, titled/entitled fore-fucker
and his screes of gibby, force-fed fuckular. His makeshift
barn bordello, his surfeit of bunk-up fun and I despise
the line from which I've come and, all the more, I live/learn/
    love
those humbly hurting, long-gone lonesome, land-girl mums...

Their phantasmal chirruping vortices, their octatonic
   harmonics
that, in their breeze eddy bufferings, make sparkle anew
these rusted, wind-smelt, corrugated iron archipelagos;
this forlorn, bust-lock bricolage of shutter flapping,
farmstead outhouses which, as buffeted, wind-scored
   remnants,
are as if rubble's awakened *de novo* with brio!
The dancing, effluvial pockmarking of timelines, such as
   mine,
founded here in such scrappy flaks of fuck.

And, o'er there, my many mothers meadow effloresce
in cobalty, cornflower array! Colour!
Come colour all my aching days
in pesticide thwarting buoyant bouquet!
Now this tromped soil and our trumped souls
bud and flourish from courage nourished
'gainst the scything, pruning pricks
that detuned our fledgling choriambics...

And, resigned, we hum-yap the marching tunes proscribed
   anew,
Scatty scant comfort; their deafening drawl, our defeat
   emergent
[via] their enfrazzling discordance,
[via] their abrasive cyclonic pollution of the soft windwhistle,
[via] the en masse percussive force of their circling
jackboots hacking gravel, vortexing assuredly for
we snivelling, twitchy few fused behind/beyond our
pockmarked farmstead's twitching nets. We, plainly
as doomed as our basicity be bound back to the mere
carbonic dust of our essential constitution like the loftier,
heftier stars and comets of the stand-offish realms above
that trill the cracker motto truism, "if you can't be Right,
turn left," *and into the cleansing line of fire...*

Village

These dew dashed Ballard Downs at dusk,
Their flannelette filtered translucency,
Their ethereally gust thwacked sparsity,
Their muted refractions of wheat-sheaves asway,
Grainy as y'like in the drawn light;
We, mere pinpoints a-prance,
Free-styling in the flashlights
'Midst their giddy levity...

Our scruff of signature left in the stomped crops trample.

We vortices of loneliness
Eschew the coital co-substantiates
Of a GPS iPhone app engineering freelove
Betwixt such brittle strangers...

Who melt for lust and pour for sex.

The top road through which we, as e'er, shuffling exeunt
To the 09.07 market day bus;
The rusting hoops of stanchions of the withered
Wreck of shelter in which 'first time' memories were made...

Cigs, ket, stout, cide, hash, snog, blow, laid, vom, chuck.

On that trusty bus immemorial, now, only e'er on a Thursday,
Sometimes, silently, without word or intimation,
Through the wanding wonk of cattle pong that sands the
   breeze,
A youngster won't return
And an aged farmer's wife in well versed, mock concern
Will glintily gliss 'er tamps o'goss...
"Dreckly, all spuddlins hath ped off thru d'dimpsey of a
   yoretide eve

Dey'll match an' hatch as t'were e'er thus; 'cordin' t'dis eye, 'tis
ne'er a goodbye!"

As, in absentia, all flaxen fledglings were wont t'do
As, in perpetu, all sylvan nestlings e'er 'av and must...
"Afore the byre's been tromped to mere dander dust."

wanna job?

i divest, you cop off: i invest, you co-opt my
self-control. your quorum queues to fuck me,
their dicks dished as this 'tricks' dividend,
i bend over for their shovelled debentures,
a floor traders' forceful squall around the
honey-pot ass of me, their faggy factotum,
this is what i do in lieu of a youth training scheme.
such commodity of body; a bona, boning,
bonus win-win for all - while we trade in both futures
and derivatives, are 'thinking outside the box'
for compound reward, as middle-managers sink
their pinks, balls-deep in my vassalic suggestion box,
spermy speculation on the company's watch.

corporeal, corporate sexual synergies,
a libidinal leverage in the scrum for my bum,
an entrepreneurial energy in their pecking order;
a cunning, cumming competency, these exploits
may not be sustainable. at a ballpark figure,
i guess i'm done after the eighth proactive penetration.
little diversity, all execs here are active,
though one *'touches base'* by screwing my face.
i process their processions of pounding,
my datafication of their dicks' drillings;
the mean, the median and modal values
of exertion, time, spendings and *'happy endings'*.

i feel *'out of the loop'* whilst some are deep in my hoop
and, through it all, i still don't know if any, or all
of this time-immemorial transaction is B2B or B2C
or who the loosened tie, wanking throngs are beyond
the boardroom window. from bestial to celestial,
I pan the room, the huffings of stuffed shirts,
a sensorial censoriousness from the sartorially
challenged; a chain-store monovestite mass
of minging suited, booted men. eventually elusive
workday evasions from those who'd, that day,
in pack-gnash, marked my rosy arse on ten.

make no mistake, this was mass carnal delusion,
a diffusion of marital frustration that seemed a
quick-fix composite, cumulative solution. potentially,
I ponder compensation for this gurgle-gaggle of
borderline gang coercion but, as the looker one
slobber-chopped *aprés-ski*, so to speak, that indeed,
I'd got the job, I chose to simply state, *"thanks
m'dearheart masturbmate! And tell all the guys
that they've been just great!"*

station

passions: hollowed to monaural.
prerogative: auto-decrement.
the register: high formal.
the response: vulgar, colloquial, overfamiliar,
a "*hi, bye, sweetiepie*" twist of tweetage.

we, untethered, adrift
in time and motion study,
in cost benefit analysis
and both conclude, "*so what, what if*",
for no-one challenges
the methodology by which
it is over before it began.

the grand hallway aisled,
in glistening, gilted fresco transepted;
the trash can on which I sat
(catching your morning-after, morphine aphorisms)
deftly ditch-kicked and, thus,
enriched in ferric rust to leach
into that poisoned, green and pleasant land.

outhouse shivers, the storm brewed,
we two slivered, who used who
in melding in the suffrage
of the screwer and the screwed?
percussive streaky rain
morphed into this mess
of a sour, sobriquet of attitude;

an unsaid, post-coital, "*I've had you*"
evident as undertow in your spoken,
"*there's a train due at 6am;*
follow the lane for about a mile
to the station, would you?"

request stop

when phrenic tectonics re/de-clamp,
seismic shifts in compos mentis
lead to an introverted drift
and/or the ebullience of fists.

jouissance in elusive cerebral
sine waves; euphoria bussed
in little bipolar bitz. oh, lol,
there's l'il snowflake me

melting in a selfie, and here's
a redolent blitz of solo sunburstery;
now, where's that *'cul-de-sac'*
wish o'swift death aswirl o'er me?

oh, lol, there!
evidenced in low-res mists
of blurry, ex-boyf tweeted,
mobyfone photography.

swipe, swipe, zoom!
swipe, swipe, zoom!
the widow weeds take root
in this remote waiting room.

derelict

a feigned matey-hatred
that we glibbed so well
in our bespoke, sub-glottal
slaw in which we regaled
gutter-heart poets whose
ashen lips were for sale
and chain-letter love notes
we wrote, but, never mailed.

all fugitive eulogists
arrested by memories never lived,
hung on clawing craws
of rhetorical 'what-ifs',
the waiting room is to be boarded up;
the rails rust to powder,
the trackbed scuffed up
with the saplings' shift into new life.

and you write with your caked lip-salve
on the cracked, mottled mirror;
words scrawled and impenetrable
about lost chances incalculable,

about your valiant waiting,
even when the first nails
to rotting frames are mauled in.
light, henceforth, will slither
but through mis-joint timber slits
and, still, the love of your life,
you think, will find you in this,

derelict.

mivvi-whipped

You furnish your realities with flick-books of veneers. I UV-lamp look at the polymer spectra in the chipboard beneath and decode a clusterfuck of *mess o'blues*, or what passeth for 'em in Redcar. A wound clasping, teen-hunk coiled in the guttering behind a burnt-out *'Whippy-Whip'* kiosk. Wound-seep like a melting *Mivvi*. Freshly stuck for refusing to fuck the mob's main man-moll, a predatory *manimal* constantly 'on heat'; orgasms mere by-product of a *mean streak* to remain *top-dog* by topping *top-notch* beauty. *(sexu-geld)*

Three weeks ago, there was a loading-bay job at the Superstore but, in another place and time, you'd have been *'an eye-candy 'n' cerebral hit'* on the literary scene in an enclave of raucously rarified auteurs, poets and artisans. Sometimes, emergent, a derivative twist of phrase almost passes your lips. It's only one more learned abstraction, *sweetie*, to make that thought your own and sometimes *'needs must'*, but, what use words when slain by *action*? What use *'know yourself'* when forced to *'know your place'*? Your life is a concourse across which others walk; malleable, you fold in their detritus, foot stomps and impatient taps and, befilthed in their trample, rot like the boardwalks of yesteryear.

But, always remember dear, I am not that hard to find...

alas, in le harve too...

Gropey-gnarl fingers pin, to piss-stink walls,
Puny forms *derrière le kiosque de glace abandonné*
En hiver. A *tutti-frutti* pick'n'mix *melange* of totty ass
Plumed in a warm whippy-whip of smelting cum
Your flake of a prick, melting, poop enrobed
As the vigilantes hoiked you off me, before you'd quite done

Leverage, with that there, flaccid tag o'flesh seepage
You somewhat lost your charm as daddy knifed you
You apologised, hugged and held me as you fell
Your *vin rouge* blood and *bourginon* shorn bitz
Pail sluiced pale and long since lost
To the *sangfroid*, saline-smelly, sea swell

chance/parade/ember

[Whoop]
Quaffed **wonkeries** and air **kissy-kiss** in the whirligig;
Ooo, the klonky-grating thump an'shrill o'**klaxon hootery**,
Twizzle, in'em **bonkerz strobes**, that domino-**akimbo
    voguey** ho-ho-ho!

[Chuckle]
We young, hung, so tautly **spun aflail**
In rotorised, loopy, **lippy-lip-synced** energise...
4 t't'floor! 4 t't'floor! **4 t't'floor!**
Twiddle-cram on't off-beat **jus'a l'il more, m'darlio!**

[Belch]
"**Oopsy!** M'shiny Umbro silks **trussy-split a bit!**"
"An' yer side-vents ripped! Aw, nah, babes!"
"Yep! 'cos of them **limbo-lunges!**"
*"Aw! Me **so soz they did**, 'cos they be verily vintage!"*

[Ch-Ch-Chance]
And someone, as set-piece 'wow', breathed **fire**, juggled **flame**:
Parade over, I'm **stoked ash**, **mid-life** replete on a doorway
    grate,
Flexi-sexy celebrant seemingly once again...

Finale flambé o'fist-bump tryst; *"Mabes see you ladz next
    year, then?"*
"**Fuk, yep, y'bet!** *Oi! Oi!* U on Insta, bubba?"

burning rubber

Scorched earth within
four suburban walls;
angry young men
act out on repeat
their obsolescent
scènes sans décor –

Aridity shrivelling
such shape-shifters shuffling
from inferred off-stage duplex;
now, as a smokehouse,
particulate scoured
by unfortunate infernos -

The week's shoebox slung
with discard slops of quim/ass,
dunked/splunked, knotted *Durex*;
the lads' sheathed cum
bubbling like kettled gum
in the hubris of flame -

Their carpet-bombing,
blather twat *splattage*
and rout, rote arseries
and no-one knows their names...

botch job

Dowel fingers digiting slack dough flesh
triggering scant knead of knotting pleasure;
culvert genitalia glistening, yet unmoved to ecstasy –

Workaday ductings of fuck;
a mutual presence block sheathed in
such brittle cowling and we call it 'versatile' –

Dispersed dispense of damp asbestosis spunk
flanged out as unset, wan drips of Artex
botch-splotched in a carefree flick of appliqué –

Let... me... breathe!

bum-fun, 31

Supra-sensual
Waspish, bluc· funk
A sex app *'fuckstrot'*

Intra-lynch w/o fury
from whiplash
gone wrong

Missed the turning
Impulsive reversal
Injurious, injured

Shoulda drove on
my undoing
duly undone

WTF, eh, *'Bum-fun 31'...?*

Woodwork

Our bevels sanded silky, knotted-
kinkeries inclined into concave curves,
all such glitches expunged or veneered.

The vice like grip of tension held us
deadlocked in a dovetail joint,
in splintering suspension,

in a web of complex chiselling nerves,
bouncing and rebounding
within our abject clamped stasis

and every affirmation mouthed
pounced on as clickbait;
reading the varnished intent within,

as ever, too late, too late!
But, oh, the smooth artisan beauty
of a man and his mate

in symmetrical sympathy,
in mortise and tenon fixity
of mutual conjoinery:

we nudged, in jilty niggles,
past the chocking blunt blades
of cack-handed hams

and held fast as our lives
planed against the grain,
our kisses in the sawdust.

mtv tattooed (EXPANDED)

Swiving, aging curs; our shags, serial spermatic stacks
of pontoon spare parts grinding, well-lubed, to their
customary spindrift gruel. Mid your balls-deep sunk
slunk in me, I caught you lip-sync to a background
synth-pop playlist tune; you and I met in an electro-pop
online chat room; *'Don't You Want Me?'* v. *'Vienna'*.

unpanted, decanted, our antennae pricks as uralite
stanchions cankering mid-life to a toxic mulch in
the marshy march of makeshift sex; your blurry fade
of MTV tattoo says so much about that then '80s
new-wave youth, a Corp ident emboss evidences fledgling
aspirations flown off with the cathode Sony *'Trinitrons'*.

That slick, hissed, telegenic *"mwah! mwah!"* as, sated,
you left of your own accord, gated snare syn-drum
beatboxing on to sensu-sexy gender-bending pastures
anew, pubic green shoots putrefy under the weight of
misdirected spendings; reliving lost dreams from when 18
I assumed, until my flat-mate asked, *"Didn't he used*

to be?" and so we, not so new romantics fudgily aflail in
our sex-life's gloop, *("wipe you hands before you touch the
discs!")* can't body-pop back to callow, cool angular youth,
so sally-on, sallow with, and without, many a retrofied,
erstwhile dude like you. *"Run the ident, roll VT, it's this
week's uppermost poppermost Top 40!"*, and, FUCK!!
It's you, the hot-shot chart-breaker; number 33 in May '83!

Bottle Brittle (The Place I Lastly Left)

Milk-bottle brittle men, static,
Stood like blackbird pecked, gold top pintas planted there,
Shackled sheer in spunk-mildewed, dank corners;
Their former 'fresh meat' sheen now murk mottlish from
    speckly hurt.
Men, bovine inert as the concrete backdrops they silhouette,
They intermittently gleam from odd angles of their tardy
    tarnish
To slag-tag shagathon, take ten men or more for the team:
Laid in relay, in jaundiced slo-mo, non-stop action replay,
Spiritless man-fuck machines dispense their wan skeet
Over brittling sheets, such cyclic a maladaption hewn
From the brassic boredom of shit lives that shags varnish

With pain temp vanished! Cuddy emissions disbursed:
These exorcised, painterly, spermy unguents, finger traced,
Smattered 'cross crispy, stinky-winky, thonged bulges
In pulsing, palling, disco-ball slathered stabs o'light.
Yet, plenty hearts snubbed here, they smulch in a rancid
    effervesce
Their indignities ignite, alight and consolation prize hide
In a *prix fixé* rent boy or two's *jouissance* of backside.
This is drive, this is instinct, this is bottle brittle!

These vascular vessels,
These frottaging frenemies,
Their vacuous hoofing,
Heifering around the snarky arcs of glory holes;
These herded, lumpen poketariat,
These man-muck spreading missionaries,
Their svelter numbers beholden, yay, mooingly chosen
In the cock-blocked, bloke-choked droves that smelt, *al forno*,
In a spunktious backroom flow atop the black dough
Of fossilising condoms that eek their steaming,
Stinky, globule gloop into a sediment of evidence

For future excavation by sexu-archaeolgists
Studying these lost transitional years!

Such filled porta-prosthetic fermentations,
These spent rubbers are as chromatic puffballs;
When flung, they transmit, as if post-coital
Constellate bulletins in their wall stuck discard,
Each fucksock a frond appending its own salacious
Stanza to the group-speak fuck-fan dotage.
This emergent tapestry, a pictogram of dick debris and
    knotted dregs,
As silent waveform plotting the modal value of a rectal
    brigade's listless reminiscence,
The latent pattern in the resultant wall frieze, 'nosey
    neighbour' deciphered like tea-leaves,
But of blood and spunk and lube and dung
And of lives affirmed and of lives undone.

Such mastic sludge mutating as *aide-memoir* in deft fester
But, "oooh, oooh, look at you; you've a phoenix tattoo!"
How apt our eyes met amidst such mawk of mid-life's faggy
    ashes;
We, a sub-clause lull in a longer tale, perhaps, than
A hasty table dance, a podium, a cage, a sling
And the sorry sodden slash of tepid tags o'flesh enmeshed in
    by-rote arsings;
Schlong, swung-slung to S.O.S. morse fuckbeats, without
    and within.

But soon, just possibly,
'We', perchance, as partners at a pending dinner party
And 'we', devoured by such sweet dreams of what budget Asti
We'd bag from Tesco Metro to bring!

This is drive, this is instinct, this is bottle brittle!

the love of your life

The love of your life
walked past you in '97
in a Hazmat suit –

The love of your life
was the lad your cheating ex
was eager you meet –

The love of your life
would have resulted
had a couple in Stevenage fucked

and not argued about a pound coin
found in the pucker of a tepid,
cream leatherette, G Plan bed settee.

dissolute:crisconnection

hope cracked asunder these hours basted
in the chiding cling of wait:
the metronomic, blustering bluff of trains' track-sidlings
in and off, ousting nowt.

our once mutual mindfulness
now fissured into this invanity of matting days:
your lunge of lateness fracturates
the staid malaise of weeks with

its weeping, drop-kicked emptinesses
rebounding on the stall-walls veneered
in a clabbering, excremental logic.
a decremental reason a-shuttering,

muting the overtures of our overages
of passé, porny love to a mere dying waft
of pixel-kiss lost within a wonk of digi-reminisce
that, if swiped right, is our only currency.

Figgy, Figgy Manquim

Dextrous omnilingus of figgy, figgy manquim
like the fizzy, kicky-kiss of insect-o-cutors in
deft sequence dance; volt-stabby tongues
lance to mince dee-lish such sweetmeat, coital
'creampie' quince with scabbard licks
to ruffle to dog-ears the crotchless environs
of such well-thumbed, aged, powdering keks
o'latex once so skin-fused but, so soon,
so loose... unfurled/unloved/undone!

Sexy sup-up t'trussy slipway's flotsam, it's
frothy cummucino; the conducting baton of
prick, the spindly conducted pantograph of
akimbo legs, the short-sharp-shock circuitry of
flash-flood 'gasm, the Gloriana glistening
monstrance of decided discharge, its leakage
from the transept of the pumped-rump ramparts
of we workday, already forlorn, post-coitally
forsaken, faux-braggard 'power-bottoms', who
are transfigured in the balming bless of plenty,
plenty cum from succubi supplicants whom we
immure with the immanence of the everyman,
the everyday, the Allhallows bellow of saint
on each primordial enclosure.

From such primal writhe, we will rise triumphant;
From the blitzoid bolt of such buggering blast,
We leave the till and toil of parched flatlands
For a quenching glimpse of the rolling verdant.

Portland / Wight Interstice

Dismal prom vista; a maul of
crisp bag litter, ever aswirl in bluster.
The endless drab emptiness compounded
beneath slaked dust slung skies and
a slatternly, skittish whorl of braggard
swash in a brackish, sour, sulphuric brine;
its flotsam, phlegm tacky on a seawall,
begot there in consecutive, circuitous,
scouring squalls of brutish backwash
that tug askance the strung seaweed's flail
of skirt to expose the snoosh of limpet acne.

Low tide; its enveloping, foamy spongoid
speckling. Its throw of slushy hush mutates
to a still marl and the child he'd called *'runt'*
throws his chips into the sea and the woman
he'd called *'bitch'* throws her ring into the sea
and the wife who was told that he was dead
throws petals from her latest *Co-op* bouquet
off the pier head in his memory to mix
with the ashes he long since scattered of
every departed part of me and all of us....
still rippling.

By This Or That Street Or Bench Or Gate

by this or that street or bench or gate,
privet channels wrought by the stomp and trample
of kidlets en route to dens within dens within the density
of municipal park boundary delineating thickets;

by this or that street or bench or gate,
eschewing the 'No Ball Games' *cul-de-sac*rilege,
the 'No Cycling' signs hammered aloft
by the *'Bureau of Cut-Throughs'*,
the riven floes of summer Sunday mirth overspill,
on overspill Estates...

just as that brazen, criss-crossin' o'tit-bits and the rat-a-tat
    of jaw-jaw
are now recalled as the molten motion of a golden age,
so are the freeze-frame, discoloured, *Disc-Camera*
    photographs,
35 years on, reclaimed from dusty bottom drawers
for the *mantle* of a *'Northern Heritage'* exposé

in which we were the *crust* and *core*;
cut adrift, thencefrom, the coltish, kiddy-clan, brick-built
    bucolics
by the severity of severally meted teen-gang fist'n'flicks
from which I still, in mid-life, twitch from the witness thereof,
by this or that street or bench or gate...

Spike Mine!

taverny ashunt in'a sordid shanty shimmy,
mayhap, the miscreants shag owt back,
the pig-bins astrewn as beddin' for the reckonin';
anointed studs spurl their dew through styli pricks
to the maidenheads who choose their groove and b.p.m.
we witnessy, wallflower shufflers gawp asinine
with halves of this or that tincture, thinkin' of the tinkin'
    dealer
an' winkin' 'im... *"spike mine!"*

soon them soused smergyforms
with their spoogey, spectral minds
are so rinsed in lolly lurid colours
they become rainbow blind
and are leached to grief's grey; latched bereft of life...
what a lottery of twists, that tryst of snorters
dealer dip 'n' dive within,
scrunched of levity afore the morrow's scree of 'next of kins'

rest in peace whichever pixel burst you were,
whichever such somnambulant bluey hues elided to anon
    zephyr;
you, now, wherever the barcodes weep,
where the microchipped can wane, wax, and warp undetected,
where the flowers of sulphur grow glowing gold with their
    plucker's pulse beat,
where 'thine' and 'mine' entwine in approximations of
    'eternity',
now, 'communality' is but your putrefactions all melding in
    the earth
and you sing, like harp strings buzzing in a late summer
    breeze,
your chorus of relief, nay, release...
"spike mine!", "spike mine!", "spike mine!"

trachea of thought

Minarets mandraxed to sloven sumps
in seeping eek to clammy culverts in
phlegmatic slo-mo floe, abeyant to
aberrant attritions of constituent
particulate pollutants as caustic as a soda
teardrop in solo wend carves dissolution
down the limestone block castle-keep in
which the jester, in bloomed ball and chain
rots in his reek -

And we welcome you to the 4th floor
of your latest nightmare in which I, as
an opportunistic usherette waiting e'er for
an interval in a continuous play performance,
sell you the out of date salt/sweet popcorn
pilfered from a *Somerfield* skip when a
pathological hoarder on the rebound from
loving the trainee fishmonger of the Nailsea
branch in the mid-'90s

Can you recall the filleted
intermittent fondle?
Can you remember the gutting
of your fondanted seduction?
Or how the rope frayed
when you caught me?
Or how the milt and roe
bejewelled the haul
we, later, could not land?

Arraigned Excelsis in Suburban Winter

The boundary of infinity, its horror void contained in an
    anthrax picture frame,
This archetypal death in life, this concrete in motion, this
    conjoined voyeur,
This tundric countenance,
This obfuscation of reclusive handsome,
This recent aversion from habitual preen, pick and comb
    in the hallway mirror,
This slipshod, wall-grip, trudge-drudgery,
This thaw to laugh at his fails, fall and falter;
Don't destroy yourself in a little bit of snow.

The pocket crumb memoirs of long chomped snacks afloat
    in streaks of mustard mastic,
The micro-discordant, cyclonic schluppety of coked nose,
The hunger it staves,
The breaking of background nations and foreground hearts,
The amplified ice-crack-alike of the shoring apart
Of the two sides of a pre-sliced frozen muffin.
Home is a hope for the future and a surety lodged in the past:
I've been thinking of you all my life
But, you're not what I've been waiting for;
Don't destroy yourself in a little bit of snow.

incoterms

There are no incoterms for smuggled, cut narcotics;

You'll pay in bouquets of necroses
And spindle-pinscher, tweezer-tease
Of scabs where syringe pricks hath pitched and roamed
To foam the cauls of laced, iced, blood on fire.

Each draw a dull microcosm of 'endgame'
That disequips motion from churning stases of
   belligerence;
Have you noticed no encore called for you,
Or your presence, or your bore-jaw; ne'er no more.

And, if your teacher smacked you in the mouth
For a verbal rout with the pastor in '84
As he cupped your puber balls
Calling *you* out for indecent exposure.

Some o'erseer suit'll write your ma 'n' pa
And say you've been wanking in class
And then the beatings will alternate
Betwixt centripetal and centrifugal *force majeure!*

And the wavering flesh turns sclerotic
And the trackmarks anthracitic
And the mind to a doughty blancmange
The flavour of which is undiscerned:

And the 'base-mix' powder tamped
And the groundswell gullies of comedown earned
And the hackling hawkings of crows unknown
Slow in their circlings, swoop in predate to confirm

There are no incoterms at all.

Soho's Back

An affray of mannered fecklessness
diverged in his mid-teens
from his ordered and august origins.

He scarpered hedonistically, flaying his fledgling body
to achieve, at a breakneck speed, a seasoned,
if barbed, repartee. His joshed victims jollied

into a cosh of fraternity, a conclave of the nonplussed,
concussed, sip-supping in one long slur between
doctored morning lattes and evening's iced, laced
    libations.

He crumbled at a tender age
with an array of ailments that afflict
the perennially 'refreshed'.

His coveted south facing balcony
a sunny place for shady people scoring,
jacking, fixing, fagging, shooting, slagging.

Vivified by a younger, last protégé
whose exhibitions explored the theme
of the remnants of their generation's defining
    debaucheries.

His final canvasses splayed with paint mixed and made
containing his older lovers' ashes and long powdered spunk
from the blow- jobs given, daily, so freely after lunch.

The prized spendings, spat into
an antique oak whiskey keg
to dry into powdery dregs.
Self-styled degenerate, out-thought,
overwrought by tick-lists
of has-been, predecessor libertines

all elbow dancing in wastrels' pulp-memoirs
on the pinheads of hell's strip-joint podiums
for flustered fledglings to read what 'liberty'
for that ageing, pioneering, dead, free-love generation
meant and still could mean

liquor, pubs, bars, strip-shows, polygamy, drugs,
conversing with hookers, dealers, aspiring to be mates
with underworld gang leaders and finding glamour in the
    criminal,
all *have mercy on the criminal*", in fact, *"reify, deify,*
venerate the criminal" as if their calling is the one venerable
    truth
for 'tis the foot soldiers of the law who be the true whores
kicking 'bout us innocent pub bores merely on the score
for cock and crack and every time someone fucks up
and gets a slap, some vicarious voyeur victoriously
    declares,
"Look, look my dears! Old Soho's back!

bully

my sensu-sexual soul soared to your suggestive spanks of
   syllables;
your sirloin slip of tongue in my mouth, your litmus test of
   the chance
of a pending *"oh, yes!"*... *"to doubt and err is to be human"*,
   you'd said

earlier, as i firstly demurred your rasped conjecture of
   fuck, thinking,
"you just haven't earned it yet, baby!" having been served a
   dilute dram
of whiskey, a derivative single-entendre and a staling
   cheese straw.

beyond the clouty clang of your trademark jabs 'n' hooks,
the realisation that we, freshly sated poofette
   punch-drunks,
fresh clobbered into the cleanse of some semblance of
   feeling...

you cannot undo those unending inverse rhapsodies of your
kung-fu kicks let rip amongst the drifts of those, my queer
brethren; we 'fuck-alls' of your touted, fated 'seduction'.

would you be kinder in a slo-mo rewind of all this 'us',
   hither-thus?
me, too vanilla to retreat or threat; too self-hating to rise
   to your serried baiting, decant the sustained *bakatcha*
   assaults needed

to render your fisty entitlement to introspective reflective
   quietude
and, anyway, your slur of apologia's a compote of
   undiscerned smerged linguas; an asthmatic charabanc in
   a crunching cacophonous cough

of gears. your *"keep in touch"* business card tamped tight
in the compost of a seedling pot, clamped in by a topsy of
   manure;
you were the gleaming pipework darling; I, your clogged sewer.

huge moment, little life

it was such a huge moment
in my then little life
i departed the croft-stead
with a heaped heart o'love
into the wonk o'world beyond
the outlying far-flung peat marsh
and found a boy, up yonder
i'd, in time, learn to like enough

a smitten drunk dance
of affectation and dereliction
coyly comatose, caned
smutching one another out
we kissed and my perforated spoils
of soothed sore soul were alight

a pathfinding night
eager beyond reason
for another such time
while I am still, land-lubber
teetering in the vagaries
of the lower paddocks
of post 'prime' and defined
by the constrain of its bucolics

i am the last of the fuck-all unfucked nobodies
i am the last of the snotty nosed weeping ingratiates
who would've *wanker'd* in former rural times
all of their shadowy, fuggy, farmhand lives

i wiped the cowpats from my boots
with the sheaths of poetic mediocrity
you ham-fisted, on parting, my way
your entrée into the literary world
off-centred, unbound, photostats

of associative free-verse poetry
i wish I hadn't, for someone said
your work was actually quite good
a yearning to connect with others
from the hinterland margins
of us maligned misunderstood
but you, the boy I once tried and liked
got old, retired, reclused and died

it is such missed opportunities
that so stud and smelt, at which
I cower in't barn loft to howl-growl cry
for there could've been a smat
of recognition, affirmation even
to know, through the interlace of your words
that I was not quite all alone as, over me
the tongue-click sods of oppression fell
like slaked-lime thrown
from the shovels of those
replete and complete
from having steered
their lives in a manner
more structured, more concrete
than us born homo-hollow
born to grieve at a recurrent nothingness
we cannot understand and yet
feel coerced to believe that such life lived margins
we'd ourselves planned
as if of our free will
as if of our own hands

i think that had I read you now
i would've been a fan

Hayle River Saltings, Lelant!
for Adam Ratcliffe

Yesteryear's fledgling salients seemingly broiling anew,
conjuring a back-in-the-day *'us'* as somehow proximate,
contiguous... *omnipastpresent!* Our ham-fisted, first furtive
affections a brazen beacon, a melodic klaxon anew! We,
re-choreographed; eloping, shape-shifting, time sifted
from that long gone hazy *then* to this vital brimful *now!*
Lelant again, and airborne supines are aswirl, though
barely discernible; they are faintly auroric in their
ghoulish gristling of these gritty intertidal saltings of our
youth and yes, dearheart, they are *somehow me, us, you!*

And, erstwhile, we were leaden sentients here, all gooey-
agog-a-long-ago in sedentary suppage of the spoils of our
Londis stylee blaggin' and cadgin'! You filched *'Cherry
B'*, I, *'Babycham'* and we, bequiffed, bewildered, shammy,
slam-drinkers howled here through our caging queer teen
tempests. Intra-tempests, silent storms that sullied so
in their sorrow filled serry and how, we, serrated, howled
here through our respective, loquacious, untouched
lonelinesses. And how, so hulled and so holed, we howled
here through modest, mannered, mutual flatteries filtered
by stoppered stutter-gobs just as blinkered krill might
tress anon in perma-gulp through the rills of low-tide reed
beds upon which we sat to say much that we hoped we
might one day *mean... and might just, lastly, now do?*

Derring-do amour averted to *dare-not-do* through rando, diverting mis-quotes of Byron and Brooke and the dissenting demur of the double-bluff of plenty quaffage and mis-aimed sputs of archaic light verse. Despite such studious deflective reserve, that which bejewelled all memory of our duelling penury of disjoint were the ad hoc solitary tears, mopped unseen, left unspoken. Useless then, *yet now, how they speak!*

Libated, frustrated; glazed wan in our porcelain precious fragility, introversions chipped and crocked and hairline cracked! We, then, faggy frats in an airless, blistering kiln of feigned diffidence and faux indifference! Our insufferable molten timidity, on its latter cooling, formed scrumps of disjunct; formed unbound cinder! We became, apart, mere ascetic, utilitarian cruet frags hacked off a mis-fired urn of an 'us' so blithely yet to be and, hither thence, that one mis-thrown kiss, *ever on unpottered!*

And still, here we are, Hayle River, pocked returnees all these survived, subsuming riptides later! I, epicentred to your saltings bound swash of spectre! We, naïves again, slunked in swells of flotsam-ish slush in the saline marinade of our choppy, lopped lives as thencefrom lived. So piecemeal, so remnant; *one the ragged, one the rag!*

And, *ad infinitum*, how soon you, so suddenly, again are not by my side! Whether and whither as ever, this nothing and no-one; *the saltings drained, the vista gone!*

archaic (little blessed)

chirrups of distant daffy threnodies,
strangulated haunts of queerish eulogies;
some closeted, kindly, *'Friend of Dorothy'* died,
deceased in their Somewhere-on-Sea.

lover covariances but twice aligned in
clammy-handed, cloistral consort; a shared
cream-tea in later life, their heads abop at what
a lurch of liberation, too belatedly, brought.

lives of omnipresent slur of suspense,
lives of covert swerve to coy,
lives of postpone to realms of continuous future tense,
their ever untasted joy of carnal bent.

their sour salved at the eleventh hour,
a first/last french kiss on a coach-stop bench;
those legions of play-act 'brothers' and 'friends'
all too briefly alive as 'men who love men'...

and only so, because your law's
fraught archaic judgements end.

orgies o'yore

There's allure in being a perennial outsider,
a virtue in that charade; the stoic bystandee voyeur.
your narcissism complicated simpler overtures of lust.
rebuffed... those latticed hufferties in orgies of queerer
    yesteryears.
was Tufnell Park the stop?

We pledged allegiance to the carnal cudgel,
took dividends in the scythe swathes of piquant fetish.
so soon, magnolia consumed us, sousing off these wood-
    chip walls.
now we orbit, muted and alone, our loft;
sea glimpses of Allhallows-On-Sea...

Chaff

The chaffy froth,
Fragments of the screes of anti-radar debris
In fathoms a-churn, dashed to smash in briny breeze
'Cross foam-headed Esplanade flagstones,
Immured in sea's brawny brio, yey!
But winds'll not upturn
This coastal defence and yet...

Quayside tramlines, tarmac sunk, traverse the years;
Transient, ever radiant in oxidising rustability
Or as new laid, sunlit, laser bright, fresh rail sheen
Keep clear o'the edge o'the seawall!
Don't drop litter!
Don't feed the seagulls!
Don't fear the reaper!

The yawling, soaring, craw, craw, scraw!
My shrunken head, pom-pom hat dressed,
A swooping gull's mess just misses my shuffle and yet....
In cooing, cyclonic collective,
In snippy, simper squall around
A sea-sprayed, smulching, loaded, chip'n'dip cone;
All hover... hover then dive... dive, gobble, gobble, go!

And whose hand then fed?
And whose hand now held?
And whose hand thence dipped?

Presently, these eve-tide shaky hands
Grapple grip the bloomed ironwork; my surety.
This blanched, sepia promenade crossfades
To greyscale, to a bleak, blank, anonymous, at war
    austerity
Where now wan, throttled gulls shed their ack-ack frenzy
To merely bob steady.

Would it be this cross-haired breeze might ask,
"Should this cratered town not crumble cry?"
I am sanguine ready for sallow tearfall,
To salute the mist, to sea-spray effervesce, to expire, to die
As, brimful of recollections oft' told too tall, I
Elect to atomise from endgame life.

Then something belch-parps that the future's as bright
As the coastguard's archaic cordite signal flares
Which suddenly burn again in sparkly, plucky array
Through all the knuckling klaxons of memory
To illuminate, strings of fêted future nights,
Tacked through all my rags of yesteryears
On which, though presumed drowned,
Though seen shot down,
I thought you might yet,
My love, come back to me.

Harrogate (Disrupted)

Viv, old trick, emergent anew
like a verdant cliff top searing through
a tryst of tumbling mists
that smeared our long lorn latitude.

Viv, bowed, your hobble stick ticks the earth.

Viv, brilliance noir, anti-light,
smutched to pulp all our early life,
my every ode of love, frown fried,
all our 'us', ever on, denied!

this is a place where shop doors still have knobs
and we learn to shut them tight behind us
and where the nativity manger is a thing of wonder
and the plaster cast baby Jesus, a sacred beauty
and where the exalted recipe for the traditional
simnel cake is a jovially well-guarded secret
and where mulled wine and stilton
in the residence of a distinguished someone
is treasured with due discretion
and where, though one merely dabbled in the oboe
once upon a long ago,
one has remained staunch in support of the youth
    orchestra
even though it musters just three members,
two of whom are in their forties...

Viv, cantankerous,
your cankerous ash interned in urn,
your caustic, hospice tossed-off,
toss-mouthed, "oh, y'live, m'luv! y'fukkin' learn!"

this is a place of treasured ornamental gardens
where the lonely feed ducks,
this a place where tea is 'taken',
where maidens can be still be 'ruined',
where men are civilised in the incessant descant of their
    'lady wife's' chatter
and where whispered rumination in tea-shops,
in semi-formal attire,
is accompanied by a pianist who reputedly played
in one of the top swing bands of yesterday
and the joyous twinkles in such beady eyes
as the cake trollies waft briskly by
really do belie
the truth that so many come here to die...

Viv! You convalesce, I scone-chew gurn,
For we, so full of play on jilting Stray,
Some other day! Some other day!

Yet, just a blurry Instamatic...
for Leonard Cohen

Just a blurry Instamatic of a beautiful oblivion;
your pulse of molten honeyed cuss splurged
amphet emphatic 'cross empathies so tautly gut
strung; aggressive passivities 'midst the berserk
crosswinds of all our jading, estranging, ageing lives.

Yeh! We who'd meanly thrived a while
decrying those who'd run 'empty to depot'
or into sand-drags and cul-de-sacs headlong,
when we were wired and unreasoned,
when we were high and couldn't know
that for every passing night train seen,
there'd be many that ran slow
and yet still made their way to Jesus
on some hallowed old railroad.

Uninvited revenants
can sabotage their deities.
Ad hoc flash-mob choirs gnarl
their by-rote chaw of your psalmic *'Hallelujah'*
as a latterday laical *'Amazing Grace'*
in a virtue-signalled, idolatrous, paean deadpan.
*(With a side order of triple fried tears sigh-cried, m'dead
    dear!)*

Their churn of appropriated *'Hosannas'* amaze me.
Their strewn, flung flumes of approximated levities
that bomb-rush bang the tenderer quietudes of resolve.
It is such, we meek and merciful fans are slain whilst
in smulchy meditative mood; our mourn allayed.

As a grazed petal in a wind skronked descent
might skitter its chapped whispers until its end
in the remnants of diminished sonant range,
amidst gruffer mauls of declarations made,
so, luscious lowing Cohen intoned, stentorian steady,
ethereal as an icicle's last twist of gliss,
his proffered profundities, so profoundly missed
and, yet, by most ignored as we, forlorn
satellites, drift half-kiss to half-kiss within
the interstice of the self-same sluicing gyres
of the 'sacred' and 'profane', yet, tardily realise
they said of Margaret Hilda Thatcher too,
that *We will not know their like again*'...

Just a blurry Instamatic of a beautiful oblivion;
we remnant cones of desiccant, we debris of
disciples who burnt, with you, in you, for you,
in the immanent umbra and in the protective Arc
of your sainted, yet secular, book of sensu-songs
that frond our hubris, our hubris frond.

perfumistasi! (hey baa-itch, that's MY signature scent!)

That pong self-rends into a lassoo clench of asphyxiant,
its scent so manacular tense on this back-room's terse
  fetid air.
What's its florid stench masking?
Piss, decrepitude or ineptitude?

*[Thwack/Smack!] Ooo, thanks babe! A meted, meme-y slop
  o'happy slap?*
Kinda... take it like the baa-itch you've haughty
  pretensions o'being!
Commandment #1: Contiguous victim/bully 'teeth and
  tits' **at all times!**

You can thank my salivating fans for the TikTok/Insta
  outreach
o'that upload 'cos rite now, you is mid y'l'il taste o'fame!
  Now, know this... in choices boudoir, closet and club,
there is RULES!

Ken the gen o'tastemaker moi by demure, distant,
  respectful observation;
panache is achieved through instinct! Advice cannot
  imbue! No ogling!
Else clawing tongue and talons'll whiplash smash anuvver
  salvo of **happy slappety**

without the pay-off o'TikTok/Insta upload.
Imitation is the sincerest form of putty;
Acolytes suffer the perennial indistinction of derivation!
Beware, the clicking sashay of dagger heels!
Beware, we perfumistasi spraying our testers
without consent...

1+2 = smouldery sheepishness

1.
an unfortunate doddery rocket is early fame,
like a voltaic whip-crack, or cattle-prod of perfunct
one-off penetration, the resultant spasmodic
aftershock convections of which pass as
a lifetime's ribald pleasure when one lastly
arrives at one's lonesome Orphic retrospect –

2.
y'bet y'sweet buttsy i'll be in absentia!
yesty, big Baz were chinned toothless
an' I'm chargehand m8,
de facto squire of the bloodied backlot,
yet, pre-rematch jitters, under the circs;
one f**k of a lossless ruck pends, pet!

kloset-kouroi

flicker mirage of vectoring kouroi
jittery wi-fi aliasing in R-G-B iridescent
surround, bound in a flanging distemper
of shape-shifting, unaligned interlacing.
a drop-kick death by fluke mouse-click,
vortexing into terminal riffs of pixel drift.

i got me a screen grab but the file corrupted;
disassocia re-reigns, the cached evidence crushed.
my word against a cacophony of doubt that
the Ancients verily redeemed their visiting rights
marching, as a chroma-keyed overlay, to apposite
Grecian porn and we all caught wanking. Lol!

(slurp)

In the covens of Gobberment, their callous
cauldrons broiling anew with pulped polpettas
of maxims shat by favoured free-marketeers
now sweetened to saccharine innoculative brews;
pro-stasis, shame-aspirant, anti-socialist, fake news.

Then, a walkie-talkie woofs from ye olde EU, *"Est votre*
crachat un jus de blâme à louche sur les secteurs de dissidence?
J'espérais un Mistral d'éjaculat de Grande Vitesse, mais
seulement rempli la poubelle avec les pets de mes poupettes.
Un homme, baise-moi? Non, mais non, mais non, non, NON!
(slurp) Un autre fois, peut-être!"

And the 'leggy-lovelies' and the 'dolly-dealers'
of yesteryear's un-PC prime-time TV quiz-shows
now tombstone of tooth, teleport up in a totty tableaux
of juggled, skagged hosiery to shoot the slack-jawed
drooly lot of you who wanked, way back, so onerously at home:

You, amateur, arm-chaired, dictator-virologists!
Scrutinise those mulched, hard-dried tissues you rammed
down the side of every part of the three-piece leatherette
G Plan suite you bought for its 'sensible' wipe-down surface
until the old sperms speak. Until they walk themselves to
nestle in the scuffy-scruff laundry box full of mouldering
'Electric Blue' vid-cassettes kept in the potting shed you said
only so the kids could tape their cartoons over them!
Everything with you Tories is at arms-length denial and
    disconnect!
Couldn't you, Uncle, just've said you'd rather have liked

a little more sex?

Are you an exceptionalist exclusionary?

I have a soft spot for the publicly disgraced;
The fallen filthsmithian, tempered by downfall,
They oft' re-up resus/resurrect within their own lives,
Their sufferance of ego and id? No more!

They disentangle their layered clusterfuck debacles,
Their once splintered decibels echoing in muting mutter.
Their discard of crackpot punditry, their wrong-think,
So newly, so sure-footed in the decrements of deceit!

The ebbing to mutedness of their palette of fake personas,
All imperfect etchings of multiplying facets of the broken
    me
I presented to you, once-upon-the-proverbial-long-ago,
For soul suture, for S.O.S, for search and rescue, for A&E,
For lost & found... for un-tearing the riven enmity!

They were not so much designer clothes
    as sartorial crotchless P.P.E. marinade
It was not so much 'sensuality'
    as a ramrod, pistoned, smash-knob parade thru' the piss-
    whiff colonnades
Ours were not so much 'kisses on the wind'
    as the rasping, shackling burn of pack-spat sputum
I was not so much a lover or a friend
    as an infinitely duplicable, tuppenny textbook,
    narcissist-proto-pervert, *allegedly!*

And here I fukkin' am,
Bleating in the cyber void;
I took your monstrous beating,
Call it *Zen*, call it *Quo Vadis*, call it *Amen!*

Endings

a smulch of sobs in the ears of eternity don't mean shit, luv!
a thin grin, ground out of a militarised zone;
your eyes, the kalashnikov-ed watchtowers
with bullets cracknelled into souffléd resolve.

the puffety pink accepting flesh,
the pistol-whipped bones atone.
don't snitch! your cadre compadres are dead already;
be asbestos, be hard and killing,
let them stroganoff you,
be man-quim mannequin.

hemmed in, let 'em lick 'n' nip
your anthrax dusted mascu-bits
and launch an exocet from the slick slipway gliss
of your privatest privacy;

change your signage from 'no entry'
to 'way in' to 'dead end'.
we've only seconds now,
only seconds.

Held to a moment that came to define her/him/they/me

The click, click **decimal** declension, pre the decimating
    detonation
The **binary** of animate/inanimate, success/failure
And squibs churning in the ladling marinade of flob-gob
    liturgy
Tabulations of tribulations in volte-face, spent fuel-rod relay –

We are no longer subject to the rituals of our ***electro-
mechanical*** foremothers. I can no more keep your
dotage with mere pawed wraps'n'snorts, or filth talk you
into implement assisted bouquets of begloved, tonged
intercourse; nor fill your trough with favourite flavours.

You're still primed with all the **analogue** vinyl carved
words of '*We Are The World*'; it still shuffles you to tears.
At the edge of what were L.U.L. ticket halls, you, prostrate,
kiss the floor in blessing that you might not be a victim of
whichsoever

deity that **digitally** hop-scotch escorts a renegade kith-kin
to his realia aborting. He'd found his tribe of inarticulacy,
its **intercedent** snap and tether, *gargoyle-alikey* of *supra-
masculinities* and, so, strapped the dirty-trophy, kamikaze
knapsack 'cross his sylph, svelte back

and hoped some **cryptologic VR** variant of Allah, Jesus or
the donkey would admin some, hereafter, polish of grace
so his blitzed splay of remnants might conjoin to 'save
face', to transfigure/resurrect from the 'zero-sum game'
dead **interlopers** of some peak-hour morning.

[See selected glossary on page 84]

uralite dorms

From civvy street
Recruits are shorn
To uralite dorms

Periscopes for smoke signals from mess-rooms
means gruel-y slops served in ladling scoops
to calm pangs of omnipresent, effervescent hunger
of serried ranks of beefcake expendables!

A brigadiers itchy-ear for cant of gobby dissent,
for radi-rebels without due credo, for slackers
and shirkers without due deference to Crown
or Country, to face the garrotte or, to shit, be shot down!

From uralite dorms
Recruits were shorn
To civvy street

yep, more fukkin' ligger estuarine mudlarks!

a risible rinse of a soapy soup of mudflat
maggoty writhe in the sewage outflow
its tepid flotsam suddy stench a wrench
to beachcombers to puke in stimulus-response
their inverse jubilantes to immerse in the inert
as shoreline nightcrawlers do and have done
in their thrall to caulk their geared loneliness
in their balming, tide-changing,
shape-shifting fuckeries
with pieces of dusklit anyones...

Mutually Assured Destruction (Encore!)

each serrating mercy decapitation
a rung on the **'ladder of escalation'** tick-list
somewhere to someone

mutated, mutilated memes in a beat retreat
to luxuriate in the **terministic screen**
of **nuke-speak** euphemisms

burnt retina blinded **pentomic** units
in hobbling kinked dispersal
quasi-occluding the **scorched earth** battlefield

we toast and/or douse the singed
in **tritium enhanced** groundwater
we'd heard their **sub-holocaustal** symphonies

of en masse glissing of staccato screams in distant breeze
of this, then, pending **thermonuclear** winter
and here we are, pissing **plutonium**

pan-sticked in foundations of lockjaw **fallout**
faltering forward into the blasted canker
of accelerated, consumptive cancers

Zero Hour, Zero-Hour Labour

Tra-la-la's bloodied, chilli fingeys whipping the placcy tray
rim for speckly remnants of **Geiger** guac or **Strontium**
cheese sauce smulch to strum, impact zone, gobwards.

On the kitchen's FM tuned, retro, monaural tranny, a smug
DJ's hissin' **proliferaton** 'bout a '**bullet** chart entry' that he'd
payola predicted to snuffle **atomically** up ye olde *Hot 100*.

Carby, **isotope**-nachos-fattened **Tra-la-la** yawns, for
it's fukkin' Janet Jacksy plugged to ecstatic blast of
countdown ascendency again, while **Tra-la-la** herself'd
ballistically posted off her *'a cappella'* approximation of a
self-penned demo ditty on a micro cassette to *A&M (A&R)*
8 years ago, an **early warning** of her talent, and she still
hadn't heard **detonation** or **shockwave**!

Defiant, she sings duets with Janet, via a handbag sized
loud-hailer, outside assorted salt-beef bagel stores near
you, overlaying her trenchant, tuneless takes atop Janet's
own commercially available recordings in wafting distort
from a mini-speaker pouched within the customised,
Polaris missile embroidered bum-bag latched about her,
harness like.

"This is what you're missing fukkas!", she concertedly
concerts, unabashed in a splurge of entitlement in that
she proclaims, *forthrighteously* and slightly foamingly,
that, *"The ruling class muso execs have silenced my sonorous
talents. I need not their mediation! You need not their gate-
keeping! I sing **irradiationally** for you all, directly and
without fee. It is my newly launched 'music-direct' service
industry for you all, my proto-fan community, to entertain and
assuage your every emosh conclavity and your each and ev'ry
niche, multiplicity of joy and adversity through my benevolent,
performative gifting of 'access to the arts for all', via my*

*supine gob and your attenuated, attentive, adoring aural antennae. So, pin 'em lugholes open, you lucky mukka-fukkas, for the fallout fabufuk-flava o'me muzak misbehaviour! This self-styled, twitched, diva-siren be-e-e-y-yatch's twist, this **Tra-la-la's** famed la-de-daarhs!"*

Phrasing and intonation as 'Sunshine Unit' trilled **rays** that **neutron** mulch the neurals. Subjected minds, their applauding hands melting, their **vapourisation** measured in the **reflectometries** of the resultant fists of **mushroom** mist. In **proportionate response**, she is escorted, flummoxed, from the spittle fried frontage of *'La Taco Belle Et La Bête'* in a bopping flail of straitjacket, thinking of the **biohazard** protection overalled bouncers, **'Little Boy'** and **'Fat Man'**, as her backing dancers and the **stockpiled** munching, laughing diners, mooning at the windows, as her newly **plutonium enriched** fans.

A textbook instigation of 'attack to defend' **collateral damage** management! The minders' **preemptive strike** against unacceptable impositions of illegal light entertainment; balladeer hawkers must be expunged, silenced lest a malignant growth in pockets of regional poor taste ensue! These chaperones of crocked croonery soon pistol-whipped her stentorian feet into dainty, silken, ballet shoe shapeliness while the latter camp of unwowed diner guzzlers crowdy-chanted, *"Moo-moo, no moo-moo! / This ain't a salt-beef store! / This be Tacksy-Bellykins! / And there, m'dear's the boundary / so stay outside the door!"*

*"Did you see, hubster, she'd fair missed her spume of lips with the **trajectory** of her day-glo lipstick!" / "And, wifey, she missed her face with the **radium** emanation pan-stick by a long chalk of **megatonnage**!" / "And, bastard, I'll wager that her acne mounds were mouthing the words to mute choruses of what, I think, were outlawed National Anthems!" / "Yes, you cow, and the pustules, therein them there zits, popped into lavarous rivulets of saluting, freeform jazz-hands!"*

*[Or did some**thing** step on a hot sauce sachet mid shape-shift?]*
[And where's my side order of planetary accreta?]

*"And, oh, zutty-zut alors, it's like horizontal lightning!" / "Oh, my giddy word, is that the sound of an atom splitting again?" / "L'addition s'il vous plaît et maintenant avec vitesse parce que we're really dry-fry dying!" / "Mais, ma chérie, tu as payé les con quand tu as commandé! / Oh, fuckety, I must've lost my mind in that tickle of **fissile missile**! / Service c_nts! Serv...*

modesty forbids

rustbucket, caliper-stylee,
tripodular, elevated checkpoints.
nettle-county sentry overseers;
social distance adjudicators
of the mottled minions
single-filing to the mudflats.

one-way arrows sign past
the site of nesting swans
in the middling distance
of an apportioned, rationed walk;
we, the Dorsetshire taser-trashed,
'half alive as we stalk'.

at least the path was concrete
and had views through the mobile homes
of those who'd once lived in the vale's
pre-fab'd semis yonderback;
all now mashed, mildewed,
concrete cancered, disowned.

such vistas make disinteresting blogs.
dopey, doped bloggers in need
of more interesting drugs;
yet, who's there to BJ to get them prescribed?
someone said they'd got them stockpiled;
modesty forbids, but someone lied...

Mr Whippy

Synchronised psyche, nationalised locale, ravaged libido;
fraught, frightened, shrivelled intellects that
piecemeal shuffle, that soundbite scuttle to
rattle round incontinent critical faculties to
but stutter in shuttering debates.

But, still, *"there is such a thing as society"*, superficially,
for sludging through the fissured mastic afternoon,
the pistol-whipped whops of queues are doing the
usual fiscal shopping trolley *dosey-doe*;
elsewise, static sentients, here cloying in prickly blurbs
   o'burbia,
penned in, prostrate, awaiting our dead heavens'
   marinading mercies,
coupon snippers, voucher vultures, 'midst mêlées of tasers,
beatings, tear-gas, bleachings and all the sundry,
verbally arraigned, loud-hailer derange
of the 'marking time' percussive tenderise
of the wended whip and truncheon clip that makes us skip
in curfews to the giggly-gruff guffaws of emergent,
emergency law-enforce who sour-face sore-jaw,
*"dance y'bitches, yep, four-to-t'fukkin-floor and sing out
'bout how you ain't gonna leave y'lousy housies n'more!"*

L'anti-arriviste est parti
for Leonard Cohen

Even within the abhorrence of absence
is a marked aberrance of pulsing joy;
we are left conveyancing the wounds –

We are abeyant to their melodic seep;
your intuit repertoire of counter-hex,
your quasi-bittersweet loll of lyrical tongue –

Here, a sallow heart inflates with hope,
there, a hollow mind tolls in outreach;
we are all but trough-laden, sod-bound arrivistes,

Cusping it, winging it, drowning in it someday,
therein be the tragedy, the mystery, the mirth;
the orientation is the destination –

For when, to a sailor, the sea is as mildew in motion,
its wonderment worn to slicken sick liqueform veldts ,
its waves puckering in indigest, vomiting for revolution –

For when, to that sailor, the ambics of trussing waves
testify in their throt of malaise; their unchewed tether
of gruelly variegations lap 'round slung, trash-forms
    a-ripple –

Pollutant detritus, deleterious of such seafarers' safety;
sizes serried from swirling particulate to the lumpen,
    sunken,
dumped 'white goods' sea-bed bedrocks of corrosive
    causticities –

We, shoreline blind to this immersed bind of junk cluster,
ever await for a hallowed sunset, imbuing it with awe,
with miracle, with the cure, the penance, the forgiveness –

A prophecy, just as you soothsay sang it, mister;
residuous and resonant, in shalom and in amen.
L'anti-arriviste est parti, mes chéris et il ne chantera plus...

Remaindered Residuals — A Triptych

I : Dumped Metallurgenics
We perspire swarf in this filings-thick, sunless nu-atmos,
We aimlessly skim crushed tins on ferric quagmires,
Our bitumen eyes dead of lusty enquire,
Our skank of limbs plated in amalgams timed to corrode
In line with our planned obsolescence...

II : Fukk'd it all!
Marly murk o'flotsam pond
with its ricochet sealant scrim,
short, sharp, snort-stabs of stagnation,
our wrank reflections twizzled therein;
cauldronic swill aswish with
industrial toxins steep-laced in,
and this is where we poor boys danced
and pissied-up our skagged, threadless keks.

Spiralised in our fly-tip vomitorium,
we, scuppered land-lubbers evermore;
hencefrom, herein... distempered any
flakes of tomorrows, yea, and singly/severally,
we abso totes fukk'd it all!

III : Approximately nothing!
Scrappy bits of scripted therapies,
their canted dissonances drift with me
like a pissoir thurible's egest of stink-masker
through faux-matey-matey, making-merry
and the comradely commensurate blast o'tokes,
an' wraps, an' needles, an' snorts an' dregs o'gin...
the denouement numb-numb afore the
unending gestalt of approximately nothing
and never and no-one and nowhere begins.

remember, pal, we were neutron stars

remnant collapsed days; these swarfing hours
weighted in emergent, impenetrably dark mid-life;
its black hole densities of remorse without recourse –

we're losing all that gilded fab of our celestial age
like it was all pre-fab, mere glistening veneer
of a cankering rottenness within, now so abloom

and radiating like a congest of traffics of taffy,
their stellar crystallising incoherence and estrangements;
their supernova of concomitant dissonances –

angulars, then, we proudly astride, bestrode:
where are they now? what is life for?
slack camber in our speculative anteroom jaw-jaw –

the tick-list cantos of our botch-job threnodies arraign
lively or lithesome conjecture as to any meaning or credo,
our fractious asses anchored on wipe-clean leatherette –

rationed custard-cream in hand, chawing on
'bout the start, middle and end of love/lust,
as if we knew, or had known, anything but

the cuffing relativity of self-serve, pick 'n' mix
deities as insurances, against ledgered debits
of so-called supplicatory sins.

but, we had once lain in wonderment beneath
a tolling night sky. them stars lolling
in their twinkly effervesce would constellate

that one cosmic moment to burst 'midst
the littling lilts of sour time left. too many
wound nuances bound within our parting word 'amen'.

and which bright young thing in a skagged tent
at the end of a coast path at the other end of a life
would give me a biscuit now for making them cum

and making out dutifully, if fitfully, all night long
in search, we'd said, of our own solar nebula
and emergent planetary accreta

and a safe space and an arbor
in those brave new worlds
we hankered for but never found;

remember, pal, we were neutron stars.

Notes

declension — *(archaic)* a condition of decline or moral deterioration

L.U.L. — *(acronym)* London Underground Limited

VR — *(acronym)* virtual reality

Zero-Sum Game — In game theory, a situation where one decision maker's gain (or loss) results in the other decision maker's loss (or gain). In other words, where the winnings and losses of all players add up to zero and everyone can suffer: a lose-lose game.

Ack-Acknowledgements!

'Yet, just a blurry Instamatic...' and 'L'anti-ariviste est parti' first appeared in the *Avalanches In Poetry tributes to Leonard Cohen*, November 2019 & February 2021 (Fevers Of The Mind, USA) and also in the *Celine's Salon Anthology* in August 2021 (Wordville Press, UK).

'Village' first appeared in *Wellington Street Review*, April 2020.

'Station' and 'Request Stop' first appeared in *SpamZine*, May 2020.

'd i s s o l u t e : c r i s c o n n e c t' first appeared in *Re-Side* magazine, June 2020.

'Harrogate (Disrupted)' first appeared in *Neuro Logical Magazine*, June 2020.

'Chaff' first appeared in *Pink Plastic House*, June 2020.

'modesty forbids' first appeared in *Lucky Pierre Magazine*, August 2020.

a variant version of 'archaic (little blessed)' first appeared in *A Queer Anthology of Healing*, Pilot Press, August 2020.

'I see your Times obituary did not take pause to flatter me', 'top atop' and 'Portland / Wight Interstice' first appeared in *Babel Tower Notice Board*, September 2020.

'Are you an exceptionalist exclusionary?' first appeared in *–algia Press*, September 2020.

'Mr Whippy' first appeared in *Poetry Bus*, September 2022.

'derelict', 'figgy, figgy manquim' and 'mtv tattooed' first appeared in *Queerlings*, February 2021.

'wanna job?' first appeared in *Scab Mag*, March 2021.

'remember, pal, we were neutron stars' first appeared in *Dreich*#7 (Season 3), July 2021.

'Hayle River Saltings, Lelant' first appeared in *Powders Press*, November 2021.

'burning rubber' and 'Bottle Brittle (The Place I Lastly Left)' first appeared in *Bonemilk II*, August 2022.

'Zero Hour, Zero-Hour Labour' and 'Endings' first appeared in *Work and the Anthropocene* from Ice Floe Press, June 2022.

'chance/parade/ember' first appeared in *Beir Bua Journal*, February 2022.

'huge moment, little life' first appeared in *Pastel Pastoral*, November 2021.

FANKS M8s...

My publisher Peter Collins at Polari Press. My partner
Gianni Fontana. My 'Andy Bell is Torsten' bandmates;
Andy Bell & Christopher Frost. Chris Braide and Geoffrey
Downes for my continuing involvement in the Downes
Braide Association. My SFE record label artists Marc
Almond & Wolfgang Flür. Hannah Chutzpah at Incite+
Camden Forum poetry events. Anna Saunders and Zoe
Brooks at Cheltenham Poetry Festival. Babette Kulik
and Michael Selzer at Kulik Selzer. Poetry pals Michael
Dench, Warren Czapa, Celine Hispiche, David L O'Nan,
Robert Frede Kenter, Anne-Marie Fyfe, Dino Mahoney,
Bernadette Reed, Chip Martin and the editors of all the
poetry journals acknowledged above in whose pages
versions of some of the poems in this book appeared first.

Polari Press

Taking our name from the secret slang Polari, we are an independent publishing house which seeks out hidden voices and helps them be heard.

Although Polari was spoken almost exclusively by gay and bisexual men, the nature of clandestine meetings of the mid 1900s, when homosexuality was still criminalised, brought together people from all walks of life who all had an influence on the language.

Cockney, Romany and Italian languages mixed with the colloquialisms of thespians, circus performers, wrestlers, sailors and wider criminal communities to create a slang to express their sexuality secretly and safely.

Inspired by these origins, we publish queer voices as well as other marginalised groups, to share our perspectives with each other, and help build a collaborative platform for all of us.

polari.com